Nursery Rhyme Knits

Hats, Mittens & Scarves with Kids' Favorite Verses

Nursery Rhyme Knits

Hats, Mittens & Scarves with Kids' Favorite Verses

Teresa Boyer

LARK BOOKS

A Division of Sterling Publishing Co., Inc.
New York

Editor
Marcianne Miller

Art Director
Stacey Budge

Photographer
Sandra Stambaugh

Cover Designer
Barbara Zaretsky

Illustrator
Dana Irwin

Charts
Orrin Lundgren

Production Assistance
Lorelei Buckley
Avery Johnson
Shannon Yokeley

Editorial Assistance
Delores Gosnell
Veronika Alice Gunter
Anne Wolff Hollyfield
Rain Newcomb

The Library of Congress has cataloged the hardcover edition as follows:

Boyer, Teresa
  Nursery rhyme knits : hats, mittens & scarves with kid's favorite verses / Teresa Boyer.
  ISBN 1-57990-348-7
  1. Knitting--Patterns. 2. Childrens's clothing. 3. Nursery rhymes in art. I. Title.
  TT825 .B66 2003
  746.43'2041--dc21

2002154803

10 9 8 7 6 5 4 3 2 1

Published by Lark Books, a division of
Sterling Publishing Co., Inc.
387 Park Avenue South, New York, N.Y. 10016

First Paperback Edition 2006
© 2003, Teresa Boyer

Distributed in Canada by Sterling Publishing,
c/o Canadian Manda Group, 165 Dufferin Street
Toronto, Ontario, Canada M6K 3H6

Distributed in the United Kingdom by GMC Distribution Services,
Castle Place, 166 High Street, Lewes, East Sussex, England BN7 1XU

Distributed in Australia by Capricorn Link (Australia) Pty Ltd.,
P.O. Box 704, Windsor, NSW 2756 Australia

If you have questions or comments about this book, please contact:
Lark Books, 67 Broadway, Asheville, NC 28801, (828) 253-0467

Manufactured in China

ISBN 13: 978-1-57990-348-0 (hardcover) 1-57990-753-2 (paperback)
ISBN 10: 1-57990-348-7 (hardcover) 1-57990-753-9 (paperback)

For information about custom editions, special sales, premium and corporate purchases, please contact Sterling Special Sales Department at 800-805-5489 or specialsales@sterlingpub.com.

Table of Contents

Dedication

For Ella Boyer, who read to me; for Sandy Boyer and Del Honeywell, who first taught me to knit; and for Beth, Andy, Hanna, Taylor, Lexi, Christopher, Maddie, and Matthew.

Introduction

In one of my favorite memories of my grandmother, I am sitting next to her on the couch as she reads aloud rhymes and stories. The memory is as sharp as the blue and green striped mittens and scarf my mother knitted for me, as distinct as the smell of wet mittens on the radiator of my elementary school classroom. As I began working on this book, I was surprised to discover how many rhymes I knew by heart with no idea as to how I learned them—rhymes that surely were the beginning of my love for words. And as I talked with others about this project, they immediately began to recall rhymes from memory, asking questions like "What about Hickory Dickory Dock?" or "Do you remember the one about the kittens who lost their mittens?"

Nursery rhymes have been passed along from parents to children over hundreds of years in the same way bards of long ago preserved our earliest stories. Today there are many beautifully illustrated volumes of rhymes to choose from. As a volunteer reader for Hennepin County Library in Minnesota, I've had the opportunity to see how songs and rhymes bring words to life for children in my community. Such a simple thing— so enjoyable and so important.

Nursery Rhyme Knits was inspired by a pair of mittens I saw in a book with a Bible verse knitted into them. As a knitter and a poet, I loved

the idea of putting words on mittens. Unable to find any patterns, I began to create my own. I started small, with children's mittens. For words, I chose the nursery rhymes I had learned as a child.

Choosing the rhymes was fun. I searched books and scanned Web sites. I called upon the memories of fellow writers, family, and friends, and together we returned to the language of childhood. I uncovered dozens of rhymes with multiple variations. Because the words would be seen during a child's daily routine, I chose rhymes that evoke happiness as well as warmth.

Each knitted item is based on a simple pattern, worked in one piece. The designs reflect traditional knitting motifs such as flowers, waves, and hearts, as well as my own additions of stars, mice, crowns, houses—and, of course, the words themselves.

The words are placed on the mittens to be read from left hand to right hand, back to palm. Sometimes a rhyme would not fit well on a mitten, so I shortened or excerpted it. Finally I added color. I wanted the verse to be the center of the design, the color and motifs a celebration of it. I experimented to find the right combination of elements to enhance the design without adding too much difficulty. The Basic Knitting Instructions section (page 10) describes how to knit each item, including how to make pompoms and tassels for the hats and scarves.

Working with color is one of the most exciting—and challenging—aspects of knitting for children. Those who are used to working with color may find new inspiration from the designs in the book. Those who are beginners will find lots of encouragement and practical advice in the Working with Color section (page 22). For those interested in design I've also included a section entitled Creating Designs (page 24). To help you get started making designs with rhymes, I've included an alphabet chart in the back of the book (page 127).

I enjoyed creating the projects in this book and am proud to share them with you. The mittens and other items are fun to make and even more fun to share with a child you love. Like the rhymes themselves, these precious gifts are sure to become family treasures for generations to come.

Basic Knitting Instructions

Materials

Use a fingering or sport weight yarn to match the gauge needed. I used wool, but you can use any type of yarn you prefer. Dale's *Baby Ull* and Lanett's *Baby Ull* 100% wool yarns are recommended. Check the charts for the project you are going to knit to find out the approximate amount of yarn you'll need. Each project is different.

Size 0 or 1 double-pointed needles for mittens, straight needles for scarf, and 16-inch (40.6 cm) circular or double-pointed needle(s) for hat

Size 2 circular or straight needle(s) for blanket

Knitting markers

Stitch holders

Tapestry needle

Fabric for linings

Gauge

9 stitches and 11 rows/inch (2.5 cm) for mittens, scarf, and hat
8½ stitches and 10 rows/inch (2.5 cm) for blankets

Sizing

Mitten, hat, and scarf patterns will produce a size suitable for children ages four to six. Items may be made smaller or larger by using a different weight yarn and smaller or larger needle(s).

Knitting the Mittens

Knit each mitten in one piece by working in a round. All stitches are knit unless purl stitch is specifically mentioned.

Facing

With the color at the bottom of the cuff, cast on the number of stitches needed for Chart A. Join in a round, placing a marker at the beginning of the row. Knit the same number of rows as needed for Chart A, plus 2 rows in stockinette stitch. These rows will form a facing that will be hemmed inside the cuff. (Note: The 2 extra rows will compensate for the difference in gauge between the solid-color facing and the multi-color band, which will allow you to sew the facing neatly into place.)

Cuff

Purl 1 row. Knit the cuff according to Chart A.

Chart A: Cuff

Hand

Work Chart B, increasing on the first row to the number of stitches needed as indicated on the chart. When you reach the thumb hole, transfer stitches to a holder, cast on the same number of stitches you put on the holder, and continue with Chart B. You will pick up the stitches on the holder later to finish the thumb.

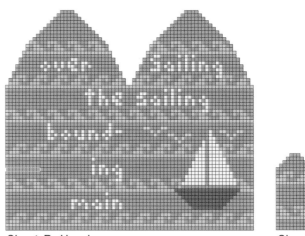

Chart B: Hand   Chart C: Thumb

Decrease at the top of the mitten as reflected on the chart. To decrease, at the beginning of the row *knit 2 stitches and pass the first stitch over the second; at the next decrease point, decrease by knitting two stitches together. Repeat from * for the second half of the row. When 6 to 8 stitches remain, cut the yarn, pull it through the remaining stitches and tie off.

Thumb

Transfer stitches from the holder to a needle and pick up and knit the same number of stitches on the opposite side of the thumb, plus one stitch on each side. Knit Chart C, making sure to keep the pattern on the thumb in line with the pattern on the mitten. Decrease using the same method as for the hand (Chart B). When 2 to 4 stitches remain, cut the yarn, pull it through the remaining stitches and tie off.

Finishing

Weave the threads from the top of the mitten and the thumb, as well as any other threads, through the inside of the mitten. Stitch the facing inside the cuff.

Following the same instructions, complete Charts A through C for the second mitten.

Lining the Mittens

When you have knit both mittens, sew a lining for added warmth and to prevent little fingers from getting tangled in the threads. I used a stretchy cotton knit fabric. It was easy to work with and soft and comfortable inside the mitten.

Make a Pattern

Trace around the hand of the mitten, including the cuff. Mark where the thumb emerges from the hand, then reposition the mitten so the thumb extends from the side and trace around it. You should end up with a drawing the shape of a hand as shown on the right. Cut out the pattern.

Cut

Position your pattern on the fabric. Cut 2 identical pieces.

Sew

With the two pieces right sides together, sew a seam around the hand and thumb. (Note: If you are using a stretchy knit fabric, you might want to use a ballpoint needle.)

Attach the Lining to the Mitten

Turn the mitten you are lining inside out. Place the lining over the mitten with wrong sides together. Turn under the edge along the cuff and hand stitch the lining to the cuff.

Turn the mitten right side out.

Repeat the process for the second mitten, using the same pattern.

Knitting the Scarf

Knit the scarf in one piece on straight or circular needle(s), working back and forth (knit on right side, purl on wrong side).

The charts for the Down at the Station scarf seen here and on the opposite page are on pages 76-77. Also see the scarf charts throughout the book.

Ribbing

Cast on the number of stitches needed according to Chart D. Work 6 rows of 2/2 ribbing (knit 2, purl 2, repeat across; knit in knit stitches and purl in purl stitches on subsequent rows).

Body

Work Chart D, keeping the first and last four stitches of each row in seed stitch (knit 1, purl 1 across, purl in knit stitches, and knit in purl stitches on subsequent rows).

Work Chart E, keeping the first and last four stitches of each row in seed stitch. Repeat until approximately 35 inches (89 cm) from the beginning. (Note: In cases where a chart was split to fit on the page(s), work the charts in order from bottom to top. For example, work Chart E: Scarf – Bottom before Chart E: Scarf – Top.)

Work Chart F, keeping the first and last four stitches of each row in seed stitch.

Ribbing

Work the last six rows as follows. Row 1: stockinette stitch keeping the first and last four stitches in seed stitch. Rows 2-6: 2/2 ribbing.

Bind off.

Finishing

To block the scarf, lay it out flat, steam and press it. Weave in any loose ends on the reverse side of the scarf.

Lining the Scarf

I recommend sewing a lining to cover the back side of the scarf. I used polar fleece, which comes in a variety of colors, doesn't fray, and adds warmth.

Cut a piece of fabric the size of the scarf.

Place the fabric right side out over the back side of the scarf and pin it into place. Working within the seed stitch and ribbing borders, tuck the edges under and hand stitch the lining into place.

Knitting the Hat

Knit the hat in one piece by working in a round. Knit all stitches unless a purl stitch is specifically mentioned.

The charts for the Hickety, Pickety hat seen on the left are on page 91. The chart for the Counting Rhyme hat seen on the opposite page is on page 85. Also see the hat charts throughout the book.

Facing

With the color at the bottom of Chart G, cast on the number of stitches needed for the band indicated in the chart. (Note: In projects where Chart G is split into two charts on the page, be sure to read the instructions printed with the charts.) Join in a round, placing a marker at the beginning of the row. Work the same number of rows as are needed for Chart G, plus 2 rows in stockinette stitch. These rows will form a facing that will be hemmed inside the band. (Note: The 2 extra rows will compensate for the difference in gauge between the solid-color facing and the multi-color band, which will allow you to sew the facing neatly into place.)

Band

Purl 1 row. Work the band according to Chart G.

Body

Increase to the number of stitches needed for Chart H (see chart). Work Chart H, repeating the pattern until the hat is approximately 7 inches (18 cm) from the purl row.

Jaxon Banks, age 3

Crown

Choose one of the two following options for finishing the crown of the hat: a traditional stocking cap with a pompom, or a four-pointed hat with tassels.

For a Stocking Cap

Decrease as follows, keeping with the pattern on the chart as you go:

Row 1: Knit 1, knit 2 together across.
Row 2: Knit all stitches.
Row 3: Knit 1, knit 2 together across.
Row 4: Knit all stitches.
Row 5: Knit 2 together across.
Row 6: Knit all stitches.
Row 7: Knit 2 together across.

Tie off. Make a pompom out of coordinating yarn and fasten to the top of the hat. Stitch the facing inside the band. Steam and press the body of the hat.

MAKING POMPOMS
To make a pompom cut two cardboard circles the desired size of the pompom. Cut out a ¼-inch (6 mm) hole in the center of both. Place the circles together and wind yarn around both through the center holes. The result will look like a doughnut. Cover the disk three times making three layers. Slip the scissors between the two disks and cut the yarn along the outside edge. Draw a strand of yarn down between the two disks, wind several times very tightly and knot. Remove disks. Fluff out and trim.

For a Four-pointed Hat

*Transfer one-fourth of the stitches to two double-pointed needles. (For example, if there are 120 stitches, transfer the first 15 stitches to one needle and the next 15 stitches on to the second needle. In some cases it is possible that 1 needle will end up with 1 more stitch than the second needle.) With a tapestry needle and the same color yarn that is on the double-pointed needles, work the Kitchener stitch (described on page 19 opposite) until all the stitches have been joined, forming a seam to the center of the hat. Repeat from * until all stitches have been worked, forming points with seams that meet in the middle. Following the instructions on the opposite page, make four tassels out of coordinating yarn and fasten 1 to each point. Stitch the facing inside the band. Steam and press the body of the hat.

KITCHENER STITCH

Thread the tapestry needle with yarn. With knitting needles parallel, working from right to left, *pass the tapestry needle through the first stitch on the front knitting needle as if to knit, and slip the stitch off the knitting needle. Pass the tapestry needle through the second stitch on the front knitting needle as if to purl, but leave the stitch on the knitting needle. Pass the tapestry needle through the first stitch on the back knitting needle as if to purl, and slip the stitch off the knitting needle. Pass the tapestry needle through the second stitch on the back knitting needle as if to knit, but leave the stitch on the knitting needle. Repeat from * until all stitches have been woven. Fasten off.

MAKING TASSELS

To make a tassel, wind yarn around a piece of cardboard (or any flat object) that is 3 or 4 inches (7.5 or 10 cm) wide. Wind until you've reached the desired thickness, approximately thirty times. Slip the yarn off the cardboard and tie it off about ½ inch (1.5 cm) from the top to form the head of the tassel. Cut the threads at the opposite end so that there are no loops. Trim.

Knitting the Blanket

Knit the blanket in one piece on straight or circular needle(s), working back and forth (knit on right side, purl on wrong side). See the blanket charts for Sleep Baby Sleep (pages 46-49) and Wee Willie Winkie (pages 94-97).

Facing

With the color at the bottom of Chart A: Main Blanket – Bottom, cast on the number of stitches shown on the chart. Work the same number of rows as are needed for the bottom border plus 2 rows in stockinette stitch. These rows will form a facing that will be hemmed inside the band. (Note: The 2 extra rows will compensate for the difference in gauge between the solid-color facing and the multi-color band, which will allow you to sew the facing neatly into place.)

Body

Purl 1 row. Work Charts A: Main Blanket (Bottom and Top).

Facing

When you have completed Charts A, knit 1 extra row, purl 1 row, knit the same number of rows for the facing as you did at the bottom facing. Bind off. Block.

Side Border

With the color at the bottom of Chart B, pick up and knit the number of stitches indicated for Chart B along the side of the blanket. Work Chart B.

Facing

Purl 1 row. Work the same number of rows as for Chart B in stockinette stitch (for facing). Bind off. Repeat for the opposite side of the blanket.

Finishing the Blanket

To block the blanket, lay it out flat, steam and press it. Stitch the facings into place along the bottom and sides of the blanket. Weave in any loose ends on the reverse side of the blanket. Cut and sew a lining to cover the back.

Lining the Blanket

Make a lining to cover the back of the blanket. This will add warmth and cover the backside. I used polar fleece, which comes in a variety of colors, doesn't fray, and is warm.

Cut a piece of fabric slightly larger than the size of the blanket back not covered by the facings.

Place the fabric over the area right side out and pin it into place. Working within the facing borders, tuck the edges under and hand stitch the lining into place.

Working with Color

I tried to create designs that require only two or three colors to be carried over a given round, but in some cases there are as many as four. Carrying multiple yarns is not necessarily difficult, but it adds complexity and bulk. So, when carrying multiple yarns I recommend you twist the yarns between gaps of more than five stitches. It also helps to twist the yarns when changing colors at the beginning of a row when working in a round. Avoid twisting yarn in the same spot on consecutive rows or you may see a rib or recessed stripe effect.

The mittens and hats are knitted in a round, so knitters can pick and carry only the colors needed for a given row. But the scarves and blankets are knitted by working back and forth (knit on right side, purl on wrong side). Picking up colors is more difficult on these projects because sometimes the color you need is at the opposite end. Here are suggestions for managing this problem with your scarves and blankets.

• Carry the yarn across. Before you begin a row, look one row ahead to see what colors you are going to need when you get to the other side, then carry it across.

• Start the row at the other end. If you are working back and forth on a circular needle, you can simply start the row at the other end, assuming all the colors you need are at one end.

- Cut the yarn. This is the easiest solution when you have a color that is not used very often. Avoid cutting yarns, however, if you are doing it a lot—the result would be bulky when the yarns are woven in and they could unravel if not handled properly.

- Work with two skeins at one time. If you find you are constantly having to pick up yarn that is at the opposite end, work with two skeins at the same time, or work from both ends of a skein, so that there is always a yarn at either end.

- Use this slipstitch technique: Work across the row with the color(s) you have available and slip the stitches for the color you don't have. Then work back across the next row, slipping the stitches you have already knit and knitting the stitches you skipped the first time.

- Bring the yarn across the back without carrying it. This will result in loose, zigzagging yarns. You'll waste a little yarn, but the scarf is not very wide and the back will be covered by a lining. (This technique is for scarves only; blankets are too wide.)

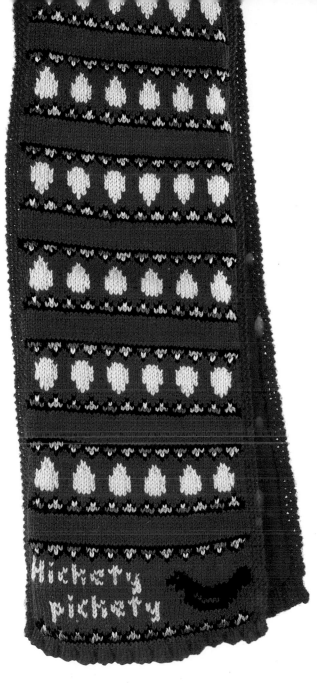

Creating Designs

I've had so much fun creating these designs that I want to encourage you to create your own. This section outlines the design process I use in general, and shows how I applied it to the projects for this book.

Be Open to Inspiration

Your creativity might be sparked by simply combining your knitting skills with another of your interests and passions. For example, my designs were inspired by my passion for words and the idea to put words on mittens. A rhyme about a garden sparked a memory about a pair of flowered canvas tennis shoes I had lost in an alfalfa field when I was five or six. The flowers on the shoes became the basis of a design.

To come up with ideas for other borders or icons, I looked at clip art, books on interior design, and the tile in my home. You can definitely see a Norwegian influence in my designs. The use of color and intricate detail comes from years of knitting Norwegian baby sweaters.

Design the Basic Pattern

I did a lot of research to create my basic mitten pattern. I searched knitting books for various techniques for cuffs, thumbs, and hand shaping. It's amazing how many current knitting books you can find at the local library! I also checked new and used bookstores and the Internet for ideas, and found it helpful to talk with other knitters. I belonged to a knitting group before I joined the Minnesota Knitter's Guild and often sought advice from local yarn shops.

After I found a group of elements I liked, I drafted a pattern that combined them. I knit a few practice mittens with the yarn of my choice and different needle sizes to achieve the approximate size mitten I wanted, then adjusted the pattern. I repeated the same process for hats and scarves.

My first attempt at a snowflake pattern (at top right) was too narrow and too small in general. I had to resolve size issues before I could proceed to shaping the top of the hand or the thumb.

The second mitten (opposite) was wide enough but too short, and the cuff was too wide.

The third and final mitten (below) is longer, has a more defined and flat cuff, and a thumb.

I decided to use a facing to create a straight, flat mitten cuff. The cuff is generally made of ribbing so that it will keep its shape. With the facing to keep the cuff flat, I was able to knit it using the stockinette stitch, which allowed me to extend the mitten's colors, borders, and other design elements onto the cuff.

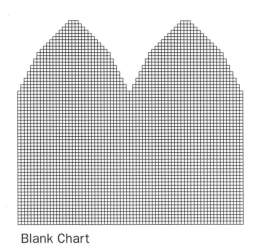

Blank Chart

Words Added

Add Color, Borders, and Icons

You'll notice from the different versions of the snowflake mitten that I did experiment a bit with motifs. But it wasn't until I transferred the grid onto the computer—where it could be easily altered—that I was able to make the big leap into color.

To choose colors for a design, I laid out the various yarns on my coffee table, or arranged them in a basket next to my computer. When I found a combination I liked, I began the coloring process. For that I used a grid with one square to represent each individual stitch. First I positioned the words on the grid, then colored the background, and finally added stripes, icons, and borders.

Working on the computer allowed me to easily recolor the squares of the grid. There are computer programs specifically for designing knitwear, but a simple graphics program can do.

Here's the design process I used for the Counting Rhyme mittens, seen on this page and the next. (See also the hat and scarf charts for this project on pages 84-85). I started with a blank grid, like the one at the top left. One square represents each stitch needed to form a mitten based on my pattern.

Next I added words, as you can see in the chart to the left. For a template for letters that you can use in your designs, see the Alphabet Chart on page 127.

The bands of shading represent a border that would be added later. (In some projects, I needed to make the mitten a little wider or longer to accommodate placement of the words in the verse.) When one hand was complete, I repeated the process for the second hand, making sure to change the location of the thumb.

Next I added color, borders, and motifs to finish off the design. This part of the process took the most time. In the case of the Counting Rhyme design, I knew I wanted to use teal as the base color with rich jewel tones as accents, and a rabbit or two.

When I came up with the bracelet border idea, I had to readjust the placement of the words to accommodate a seven-row border instead of the four rows I had originally planned. This worked because there were only three bands of words with plenty of room above and below to expand. Two rows had to be added to the cuff to fit both the rabbit motif and the bracelet border. Again, charts for both hands had to be altered.

Knit and Knit Again

When I reached the knitting stage of the various projects for the book, I immediately found that my "perfect" designs had flaws— the edge of the scarf or mitten cuff wouldn't lay flat; the rhyme began on the right-hand mitten when it should have been on the left hand; the thumb was covering the words; the hat was too small.

Sometimes I ripped it out and other times I kept the partially knitted item to compare to the next one. Each problem had to be resolved, the pattern and grids revised, and the knitting begun all over again.

Once I was satisfied with the patterns and confident that other knitters would be able to follow them successfully, I enlisted friends to test my patterns and help with the knitting. I was shocked by the number of flaws they discovered and what things they found unclear.

I modified the instructions and the individual charts to correct the errors and to make the designs easier to knit. For example, the test knitters found it frustrating to carry multiple colors, especially having to pick up a color that is at the opposite end when working back and forth. So I added the Working with Color section (page 22), that includes tips for managing that problem. The charts were modified to include the number of stitches to cast on or increase, and thumb charts were added.

Keeping a record of the changes I made as the designs evolved proved invaluable. For example, after many attempts to form the crown of a hat, I was grateful for the reminder that I decreased on the second, fourth, sixth, and seventh rows to achieve the results I liked best.

Eventually the problems were worked out and all my designs became real three-dimensional mittens, hats, scarves, and blankets. How gratifying it was to see the actual, physical result of the creative process.

Add the Finishing Touches

Blocking, weaving in ends, sewing cuffs, making linings, and creating embellishments such as pompoms and tassels are little details that help your finished product make a big impression.

I decided to line my mittens because there were so many loops inside the mittens, little fingers would surely get tangled in them. Linings were also added to cover the backside of the knitting on the scarves. The linings looked great, added warmth, and contributed to a higher-quality product.

Sure, this is a lot of work, but in the end you'll have something that only you could have created.

General Design Tips

• Be sure to place words, icons, or primary design elements where they will stand out; avoid placing them along seams or behind a thumb.

• Try to avoid placing multiple colors or icons where rows are decreasing, as it is more difficult to work with multiple yarns and keep a smooth tension.

• Use strongly contrasting colors where design elements overlap or appear side by side. For example, an orange star on a red background is not going to appear as clearly as a yellow or white star.

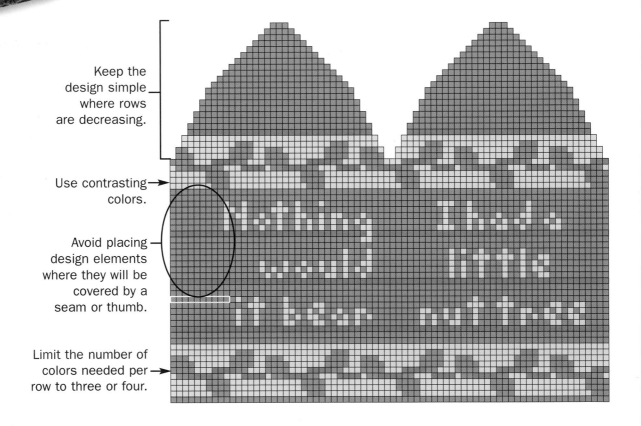

Keep the design simple where rows are decreasing.

Use contrasting colors.

Avoid placing design elements where they will be covered by a seam or thumb.

Limit the number of colors needed per row to three or four.

- Motifs that repeat at regular intervals are easier to knit and appear more smooth than random icons or design elements. For example, in Sailing (page 38) design the waves are far easier to knit than the sailboat.

- Limit the number of colors needed for a given row to three or four. Carrying multiple yarns adds complexity and bulk. Plus it can be hard to juggle all those yarns and keep them from getting tangled.

- Avoid pattern elements that require picking up yarn from the opposite end of a row if working back and forth. (This is not an issue when working in a round.) For example, if you are making a scarf with colored bands, using an even number of rows for each color will ensure that the yarn will be waiting at the proper end the next time you need it.

About the Projects

On the following pages you'll find knitting projects based on 16 nursery rhymes, which include 14 ensembles for hats, scarves, and/or mittens, and two baby blankets. Each project contains all the charts needed to make each item in the photographs. The approximate amount of yarn you'll need for each color is indicated in the color key. All measurements are given in U.S. with the metric equivalent in parentheses.

Throughout the book, I've included extra tips about knitting, designing, the history of certain rhymes, and the joy of reading to children. Remember that there's an alphabet chart in the back of the book, and feel free to use it to make your own designs.

May you have as much fun with *Nursery Rhyme Knits* as I did—good luck!

Ring Around the Roses

Ring around the roses
A pocket full of posies
A-tishoo! A-tishoo!
We all fall down!

Ring Around the Roses

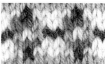 Roses. Rosy. Rosies. You may have sung a different version (I chose a British one), but whatever wording you prefer, you're sure to remember dancing hand-in-hand in a circle and then dropping all together to the ground. The rose border in this joyful design was inspired by the 1930s tiles around my hearth. The dark green rings, stripes, and words brighten the design by providing contrast to the yellow and pink background.

Carmin Charen, age 5

Mittens

- ☐ Med. Pink (150 g)
- ☐ Lt. Yellow (100 g)
- ■ Dk. Green (100 g)
- ■ Dk. Pink (50 g)

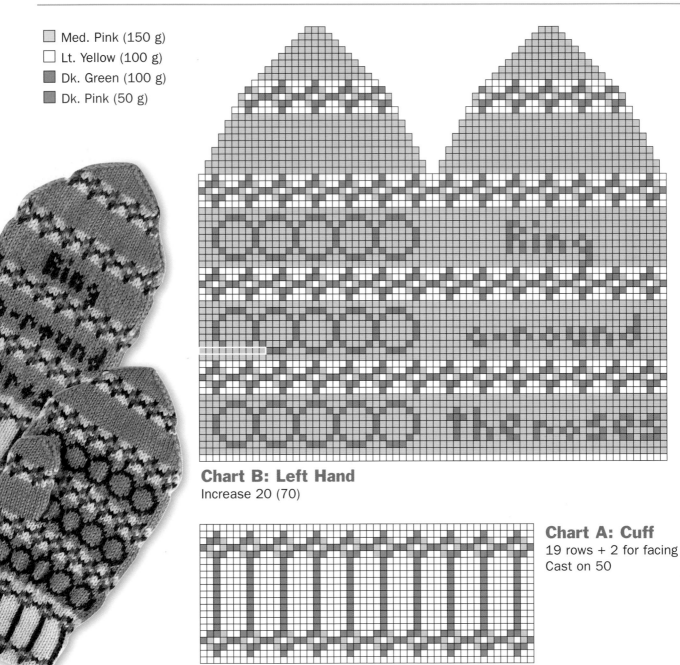

Chart B: Left Hand
Increase 20 (70)

Chart A: Cuff
19 rows + 2 for facing
Cast on 50

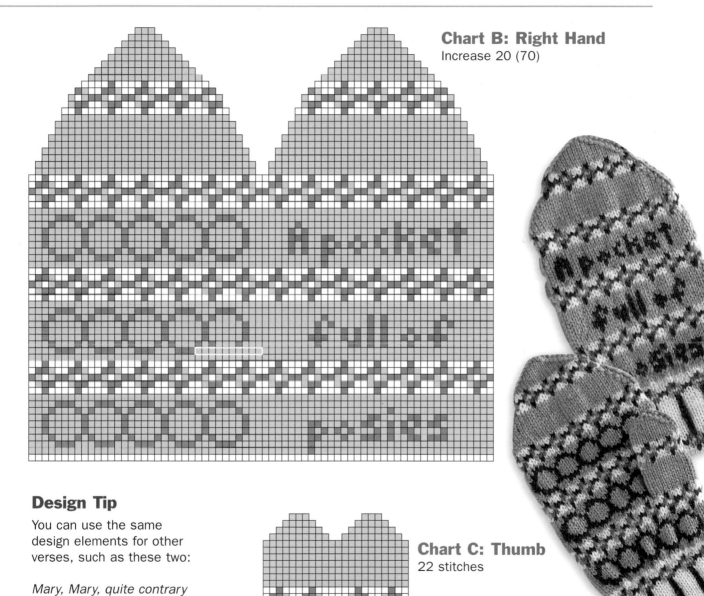

Chart B: Right Hand
Increase 20 (70)

Design Tip

You can use the same design elements for other verses, such as these two:

Mary, Mary, quite contrary
How does your garden grow?

March winds and April showers
Bring forth May flowers

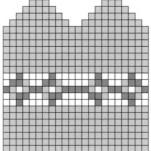

Chart C: Thumb
22 stitches

Scarf

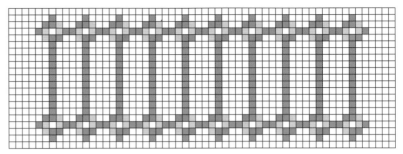

Chart D: Scarf
Cast on 58

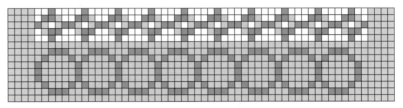

Chart E: Scarf

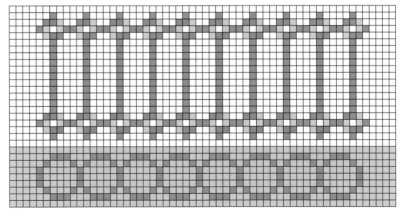

Chart F: Scarf

Design Tip

The rose border on the scarf is tricky to knit because the dark pink and dark green colors appear every other row. It's not a problem for the hat or mittens because they are knitted in a round, but since the scarf is knitted back and forth, the pink and green yarns always end up on the opposite end from where they are needed. Try working with two skeins of each color at the same time, or use the slipstitch technique. See Working with Color (page 22) for further details and other solutions to this common problem.

Hat

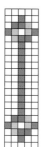

Chart G: Band
21 rows + 2 for facing
Cast on 180

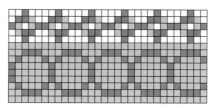

Chart H: Hat
No Increase (180)

Ring Around the Roses

You may know this rhyme in its popular American version:

Ring around the rosie
A pocketful of posie
Ashes! Ashes!
We all fall down

The word "fall" goes back to nineteenth-century England, meaning bow or curtsey. Folklorists theorize the rhyme was sung as part of a ring game played at parties in place of traditional dances which had been banned for religious reasons. Children joined hands in a ring as part of the game.

Sailing

Sailing, sailing, over the bounding main
For many a stormy wind shall blow
E'er Jack comes home again

Oh, sailing, sailing, over the bounding main
For many a stormy wind shall blow
E'er Jack comes home again

Sailing

I wasn't familiar with this rhyme before creating this book. I passed over it several times and didn't even recognize it when my mom sang it to me. I said, "Did you make that up?" and she replied, "Honey, I'm not that good." It was the perfect rhyme for a wave motif, and I loved the idea of a summer theme on winter knitwear. The sailboat is challenging, but worth your patience, and once you get beyond it, the knitting will go quickly.

Evan Rhatigan, age 2½

Mittens

Chart B: Left Hand
Increase 24 (72)

Chart A: Left Cuff
20 rows + 2 for facing
Cast on 48

Chart C: Left Thumb
22 stitches

- ▆ Med. Blue (200 g)
- ☐ Aqua (50 g)
- ▆ Dk. Blue (50 g)
- ☐ Lt. Blue (50 g)
- ☐ Off-White (50 g)
- ▆ Orange (50 g)

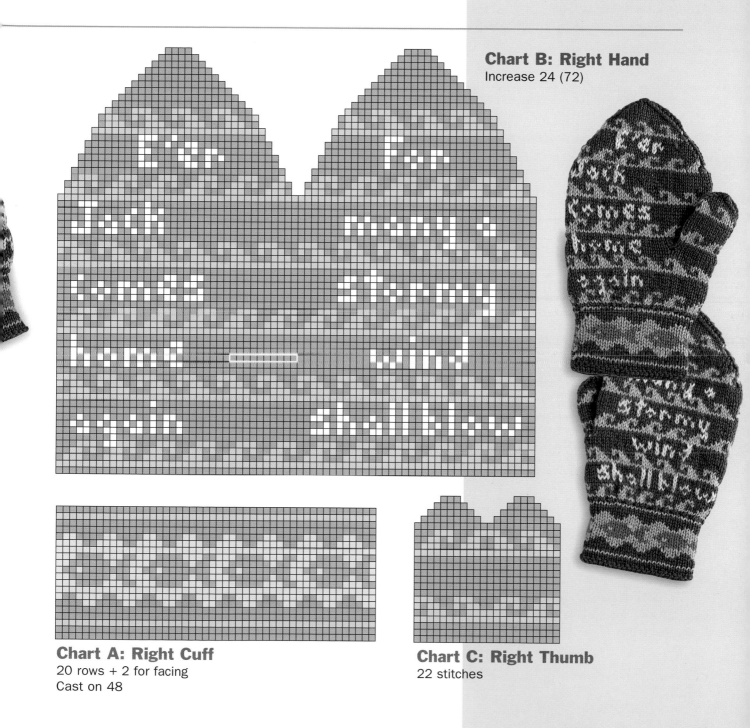

Chart B: Right Hand
Increase 24 (72)

Chart A: Right Cuff
20 rows + 2 for facing
Cast on 48

Chart C: Right Thumb
22 stitches

Scarf

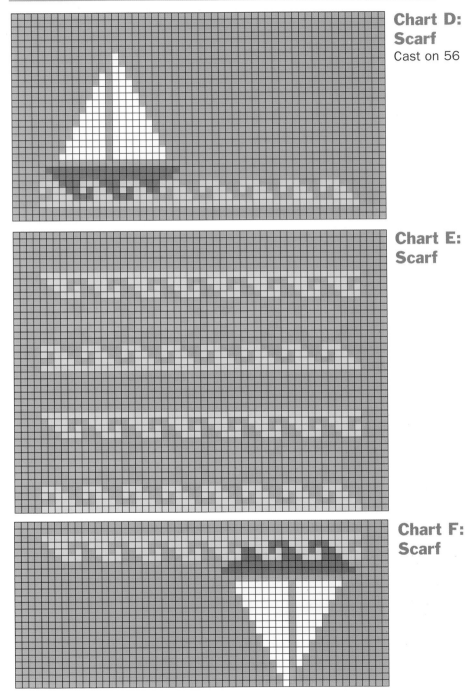

**Chart D:
Scarf**

Cast on 56

**Chart E:
Scarf**

**Chart F:
Scarf**

Design Tip

A lovely way to personalize the scarf would be to embroider your child's name on the ends. Kids love clothing that shows off their names. And it's a good way to ensure the scarf has a good chance of coming home if it's lost!

Hat

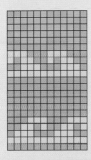

Sailing Sailing over the bounding main

Chart G: Band

22 rows + 2 for facing
Cast on 174
(Note: Repeat the small section
of the chart (above far right)
4 times before and after the
longer section.)

Chart H: Hat

Increase 6 (180)

Design Tip

Here's how to turn this design into a blanket. Follow the basic knitting instructions for blankets, (see page 20), using Sailing Charts G and H in place of Blanket Chart A. After knitting Chart G, continue with Chart H, repeating 12 times, or until you have reached a suitable length, then work Chart G again (upside down this time). For the side borders, use Chart G again, extending it 30 or more stitches, depending upon the length of your blanket.

Sleep Baby Sleep

Sleep, baby, sleep
Thy papa guards the sheep
Thy mama shakes the dreamland tree
And from it fall sweet dreams for thee
Sleep, baby, sleep

Sleep, baby, sleep
Our cottage vale is deep
The little lamb is on the green
With woolly fleece so soft and clean
Sleep, baby, sleep

Sleep, baby, sleep
Down where the woodbines creep
Be always like the lamb so mild
A kind and sweet and gentle child
Sleep, baby, sleep

Sleep Baby Sleep

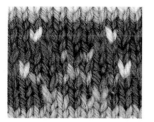

This verse was the natural choice for a blanket. I'm not sure of its origin or the original sequence of verses, but I am sure that the pastoral sheep and blossoming flower borders set a mood perfect for napping. Soft yellow and blue backgrounds suit both boys and girls. The blanket is big enough to cover an infant or car seat, and small enough to carry for comfort when traveling away from home.

Maggie Rhatigan, age 5 months

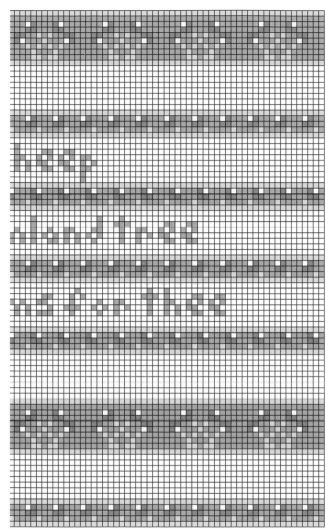

Chart A: Main Blanket – Top

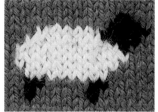

Design Tip

To add length to the blanket, add a row or two of yellow above and below each row of words. You'll need to increase the length of Chart B and add a skein of yellow yarn, but the solid-colored rows are quick and easy to knit.

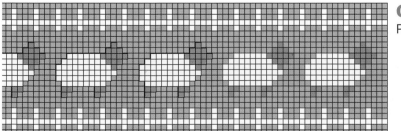

Chart B: Side Border

Pick up 182 stitches

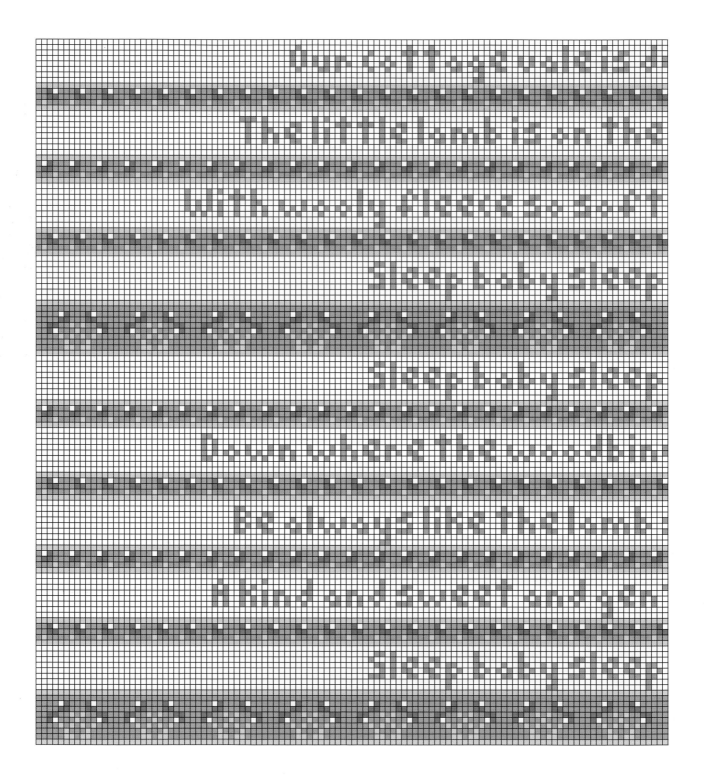

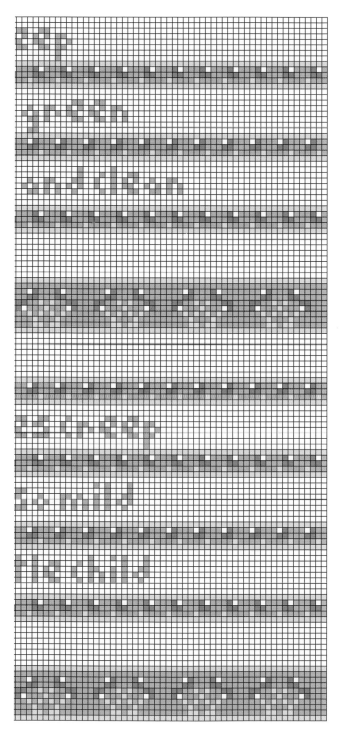

Chart A: Main Blanket - Bottom
Cast on 170

Design Tip

To produce a lovely frame around the vale "where the woodbines creep," carry the sheep borders across the top and bottom as well as the sides. Simply add Chart B to the top and bottom of Chart A. You'll have to deduct 11 stitches to make it fit across, so omit one of the sheep and leave four columns of blue at both ends of the border. You'll also need to add two sheep to Chart B plus a few extra blue columns at both ends when you work the side borders. Be sure to buy a couple extra skeins of blue yarn.

Twinkle, Twinkle, Little Star

Twinkle, twinkle, little star
How I wonder what you are
Up above the world so high
Like a diamond in the sky
Twinkle, twinkle, little star
How I wonder what you are!

Twinkle, Twinkle, Little Star

 This endearing little rhyme was my first design. Inspired by the colorful bits of leftover yarn in my collection, I decided to use them all! The background and stripes have a denim look and the colorful words and star icons blend beautifully. This deceptively simple design is a great choice for those who are new to working with color.

Chavis Williams, age 5

Mittens

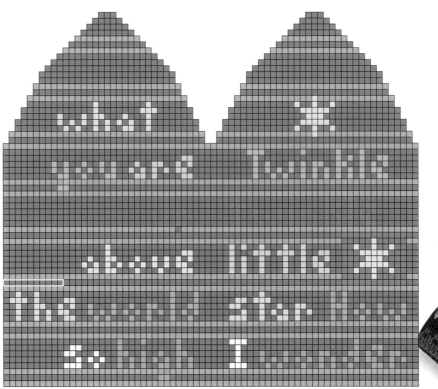

Chart B: Left Hand
Increase 20 (70)

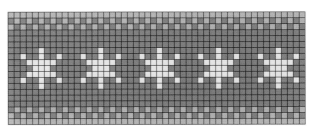

Chart A: Cuff
19 rows + 2 for facing
Cast on 50

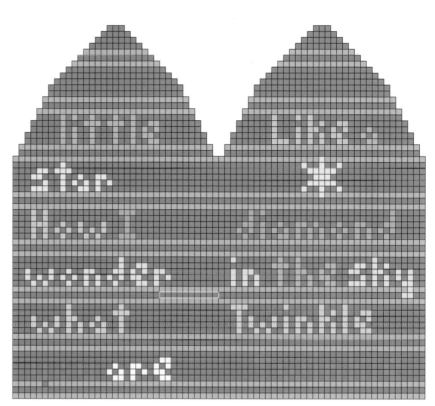

Chart B: Right Hand
Increase 20 (70)

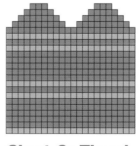

Chart C: Thumb
22 stitches

■ Dk. Blue (150 g)   □ Lt. Blue (50 g)
■ Med. Blue (100 g) ■ Orange (50 g)
□ Gold (50 g)   □ Lt. Yellow (50 g)
■ Red (50 g)   ■ Teal (50 g)
■ Lavender (50 g)   ■ Dk. Pink (50 g)
□ Green (50 g)

Scarf

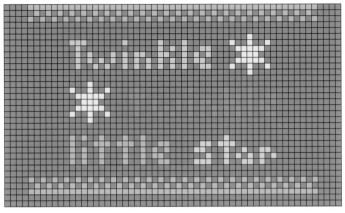

Chart D: Scarf

Cast on 57

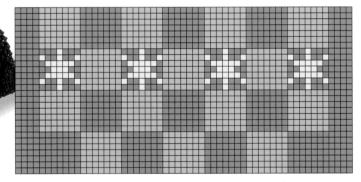

Chart E: Scarf

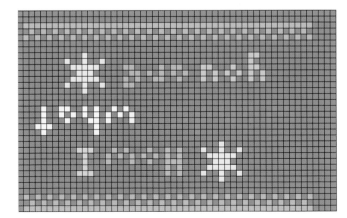

Chart F: Scarf

Hat

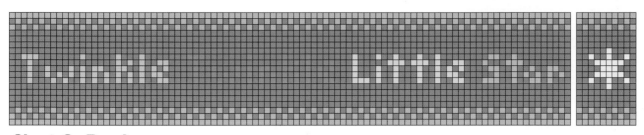

Chart G: Band

19 rows + 2 for facing
Cast on 175
(Note: Repeat the small section of
the chart with the star icon (above
far right) 4 times before and after
the longer section.)

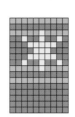

Chart H: Hat

Increase 5 (180)

Design Tip

The hat band (Chart G) for this design is the
most difficult element because of the six colors you have to carry to knit the words. An
easy alternative, especially for beginners, is to
knit the band but omit the words, then use
duplicate stitch to embroider the words
later. Work slowly, matching the gauge
as you go, and don't pull your thread
too tight. No one will ever know
you added the words later!

Mary Had a Little Lamb

Mary had a little lamb
With fleece as white as snow
Everywhere that Mary went
The lamb was sure to go

It followed her to school one day
Which was against the rules
It made the children laugh and play
To see a lamb at school

Mary Had a Little Lamb

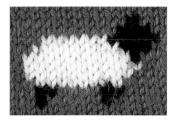

The fashionable green and pink color combination in this design, which was inspired by the classic children's song, is sure to catch the attention of little girls everywhere. The sweet pink rosebuds and woolly white sheep are pretty irresistible, too. The fact that the mittens are knit with wool yarn makes the sheep all the more dear.

Kayleigh Rhatigan, age 5

Mittens

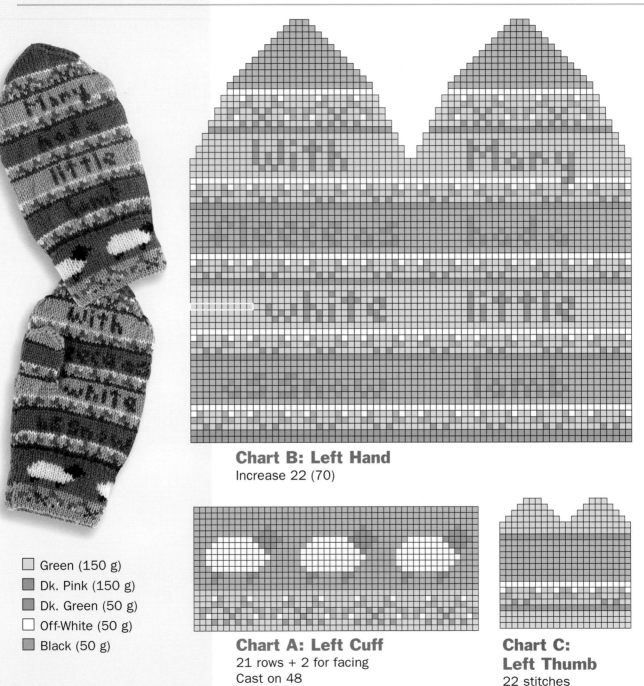

Chart B: Left Hand
Increase 22 (70)

Green (150 g)
Dk. Pink (150 g)
Dk. Green (50 g)
Off-White (50 g)
Black (50 g)

Chart A: Left Cuff
21 rows + 2 for facing
Cast on 48

**Chart C:
Left Thumb**
22 stitches

Chart B: Right Hand
Increase 22 (70)

Chart A: Right Cuff
21 rows + 2 for facing
Cast on 48

**Chart C:
Right Thumb**
22 stitches

Scarf

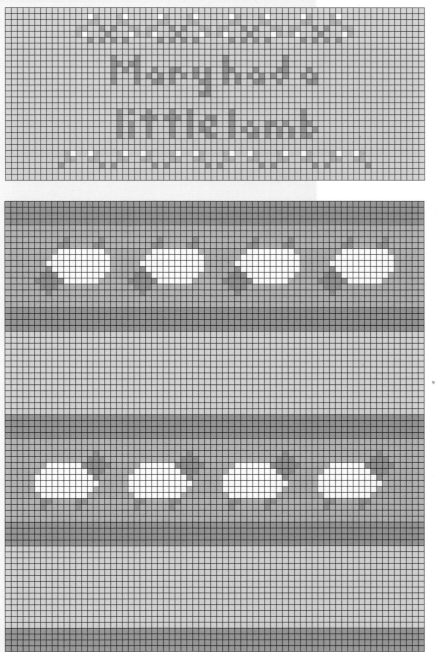

Chart D: Scarf

Cast on 71

Chart E: Scarf

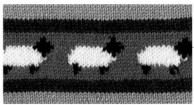

Mary Had
a Little Lamb

Mary Had a Little Lamb is the true story of a girl from Massachusetts named Mary Sawyer who nursed a sick lamb back to heath. In return the lamb became her pet and followed her everywhere—including to school.

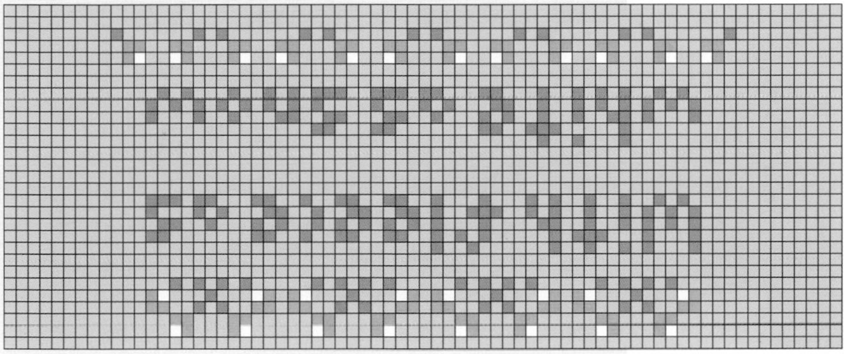

Chart F: Scarf

Hat

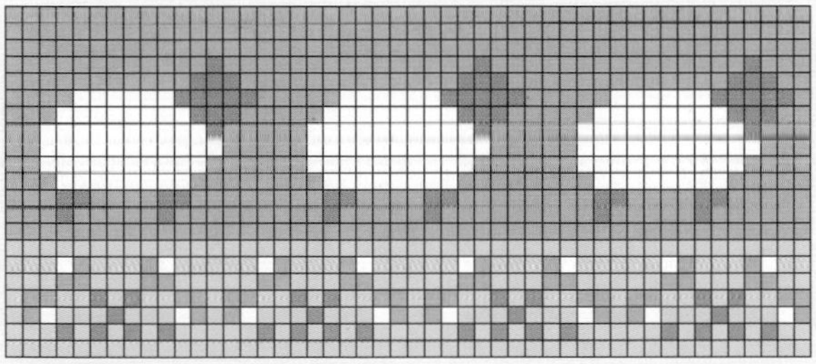

Chart G: Band
22 rows + 2 for facing
Cast on 192

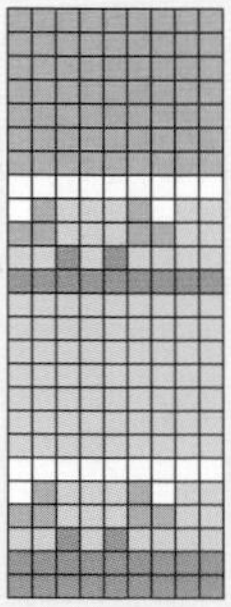

Chart H: Hat
Increase 6 (198)

Hickory, Dickory, Dock

Hickory, dickory, dock
The mouse ran up the clock
The clock struck one
The mouse ran down
Hickory, dickory, dock

Hickory, Dickory, Dock

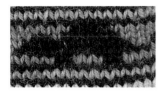

This is a fun rhyme to read aloud. To capture the liveliness of clocks ticking, mice scampering, and the up-and-down, back-and-forth movements, I scattered the words, strategically positioned the mice in both directions, and used lots of color. I am especially fond of the grandfather clock, which is not easy to knit, but if you take your time you'll love the results. I was having so much fun that I added pompoms to the four-pointed hat and the scarf.

Emily White, age 4

Mittens

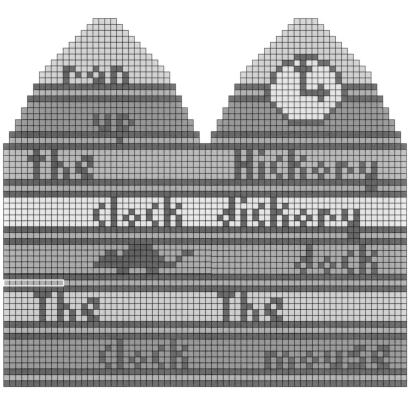

Chart B: Left Hand
Increase 20 (68)

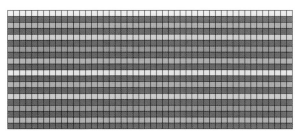

Chart A: Cuff
20 rows + 2 for facing
Cast on 48

■ Black (100 g)
■ Med. Blue (50 g)
□ Green (50 g)
■ Dk. Pink (50 g)
□ Gold (50 g)
■ Lavender (50 g)
■ Orange (50 g)

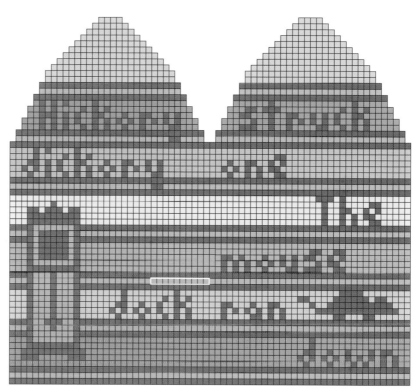

Chart B: Right Hand
Increase 20 (68)

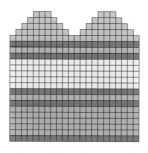

Chart C: Thumb
22 stitch

Hickory Dickory Dock

There are many theories about the meaning of this rhyme. My favorite is that the words "hickory," "dickory," and "dock" came from Celtic words for numbers used by medieval shepherds to count their flock, and then again to "count sheep" with their children when putting them to sleep.

Scarf

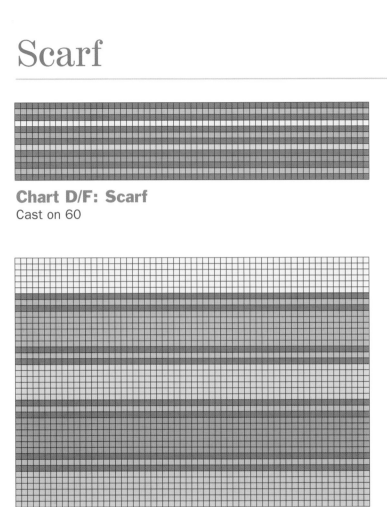

Chart D/F: Scarf
Cast on 60

Chart E: Scarf

Reading to Children

Picture books with nursery rhymes are great conversation starters with children. You might want to ask a child if she knows the rhyme before you read it, so that you can say it together. Then, if there's a picture, you can talk about it before saying the words again. Children will pick out the tiniest details in a picture, giving you a chance to reinforce vocabulary or ask questions.

Hat

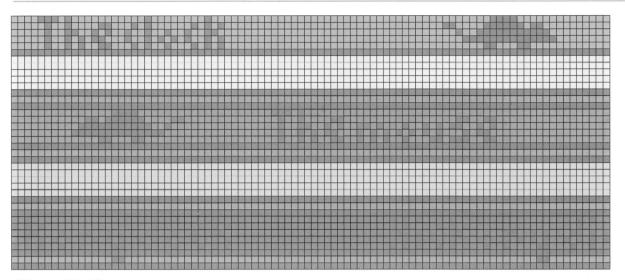

Chart H: Hat

No increase (180)

(Note: Repeat the chart to get 180 stitches.)

Chart G: Band

20 rows + 2 for facing
Cast on 180

Design Tip

For help making tassels, pompoms, cords, and other potential finishing items, check your local craft or yarn store for tools or kits. I found an inexpensive, plastic tool for making pompoms that saved me the grief of having to cut out a cardboard template that would undoubtedly need replacing after a few uses.

I Had a Little Nut Tree

I had a little nut tree
Nothing would it bear
But a silver nutmeg
And a golden pear

The King of Spain's daughter
Came to visit me
And all for the sake
Of my little nut tree

I skipped over water
I danced over sea
And all the birds in the air
Couldn't catch me

I Had a Little Nut Tree

When I originally chose this rhyme I had a pine tree design in mind. But, after working with it, I ended up with something completely different—the branch and leaf border. The more up-close view provides a fitting background for the discovery of the nutmeg and pear icons. I love the woodsy green and brown colors with yellow and white accents.

Evan Neel, age 4

Mittens

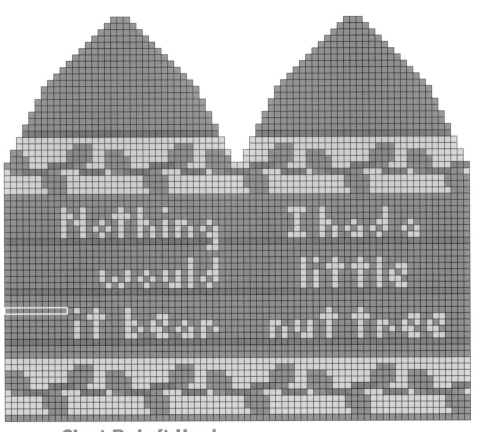

Chart B: Left Hand
Increase 10 (74)

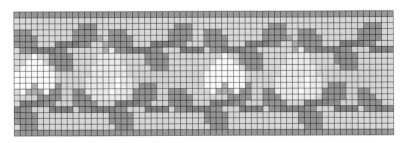

Chart A: Cuff
21 rows + 2 for facing
Cast on 64

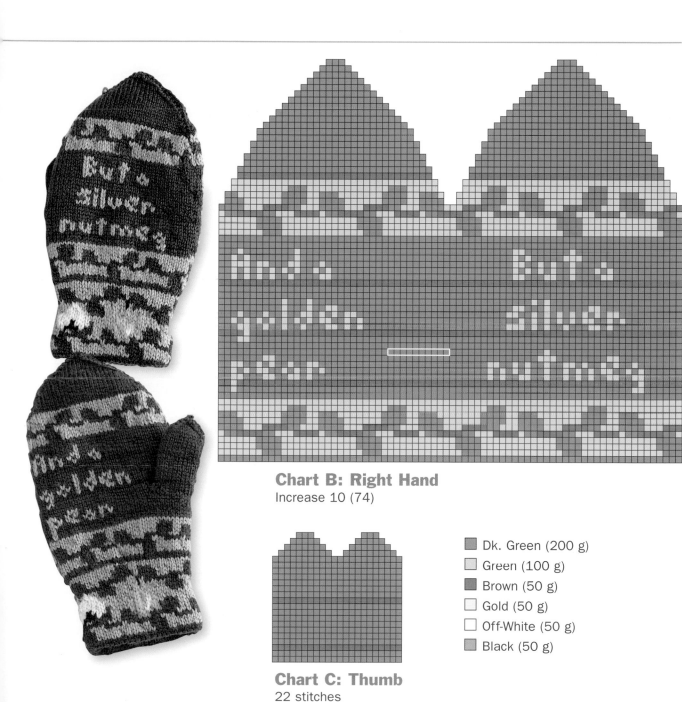

Chart B: Right Hand
Increase 10 (74)

Chart C: Thumb
22 stitches

■ Dk. Green (200 g)
□ Green (100 g)
■ Brown (50 g)
□ Gold (50 g)
□ Off-White (50 g)
■ Black (50 g)

Scarf

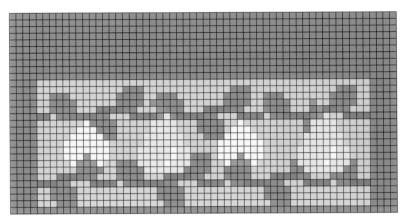

Chart D: Scarf
Cast on 58

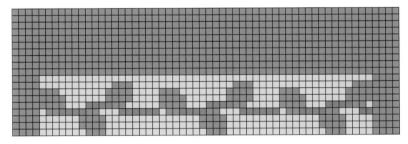

Chart E: Scarf

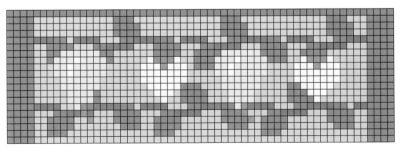

Chart F: Scarf

I Had a Little Nut Tree

The gold pear and silver nutmeg in this poem are said to be gifts tied to a tree in the garden of Versailles. They were presented to the daughter of a French prince by a Spanish prince when the two children were betrothed at the age of six or seven. They had a very happy first acquaintance and were later married at the age of 15.

Hat

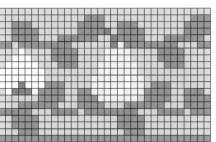

Chart G: Band
Cast on 192

Chart H: Hat
No increase (192)

Design Tip

The branch border at the top of the stocking cap is somewhat hidden in the gathered shape of the crown. While the repeated pattern unifies it with the other items in this ensemble, the pear and nutmeg border is striking enough that you could omit the top nine rows of Chart H and knit the crown of the hat in a simple, solid dark green with brown stripes.

Down at the Station

Down at the station
Early in the morning
See the little puffer-billies
All in a row
See the engine driver
Pull his little lever
Puff, puff, peep, peep
Off we go!

Down at the Station

These cheerful little puffer-billies would brighten any child's winter apparel. The verse is positioned on the scarf to be read from the center down both sides with the caboose and engine flanking each end. I knit it in one piece simply by turning the chart upside down to knit the second half. You could also knit each side separately and join them using the Kitchener stitch, leaving no seam. The cap duplicates the track motif in bands of color.

Evan Neel, age 4

Scarf

Chart D: Scarf

Cast on 64

Chart E: Scarf – Top

Design Tip

Charts E of this design require you to knit the charts, turn them upside down, and knit them again. The result is that the verses on both sides of the scarf are right-side-up, making it easy to read them when the scarf is worn. Another option is to knit Charts D and E in one piece and Charts F and E in one piece, and then join the tops together using the Kitchener stitch. Make sure you don't bind off! You'll need the last row of stitches for each piece on a straight needle to do this. Directions for the Kitchener stitch can be found under Knitting the Hat on page 19.

Chart F: Scarf

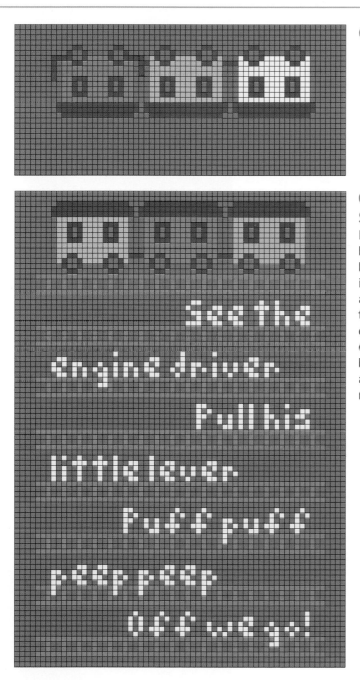

Chart E: Scarf – Bottom

Knit all of Chart E, both top and bottom, then turn it upside down and repeat. On the second set of train cars, use different colors; blue, orange, and yellow are recommended.

Hat

Chart G: Band
20 rows + 2 for facing
Cast on 180

Chart H: Hat
No increase (180)

- Dk. Blue (150 g)
- Red (100 g)
- Med. Blue (50 g)
- Gold (50 g)
- Black (50 g)
- Off-White (50 g)
- Orange (50 g)
- Teal (50 g)
- Purple (50 g)
- Green (50 g)

Design Tip

Earflaps are a warm extra touch if this hat is for a baby. Pick up 30 stitches on the right side of the hat. (This is really easy along that purled edge.) Work in garter stitch for 1½ inches (3.8 cm), then decrease along each edge every other row until only 4 stitches remain. Continue working those 4 stitches in garter stitch until you've knitted a section long enough to work as a tie, then bind off. Repeat on the left side of the hat.

Counting Rhyme

1, 2, 3, 4, 5
I caught a hare alive
6, 7, 8, 9, 10
I let her go again

Counting Rhyme

I call this counting rhyme my bracelet design, because the red and purple squares are like gems framed in aqua and strung on a string—and it was the rich jewel tones of the red, purple, and teal yarns that inspired me. The squares are fun to count, so on the scarf and hat I added larger squares containing numbers. The white rabbits bring the rhyme to life and provide a refreshing contrast to the darker, bolder colors.

Margaret Rose Murphy, age 4

Mittens

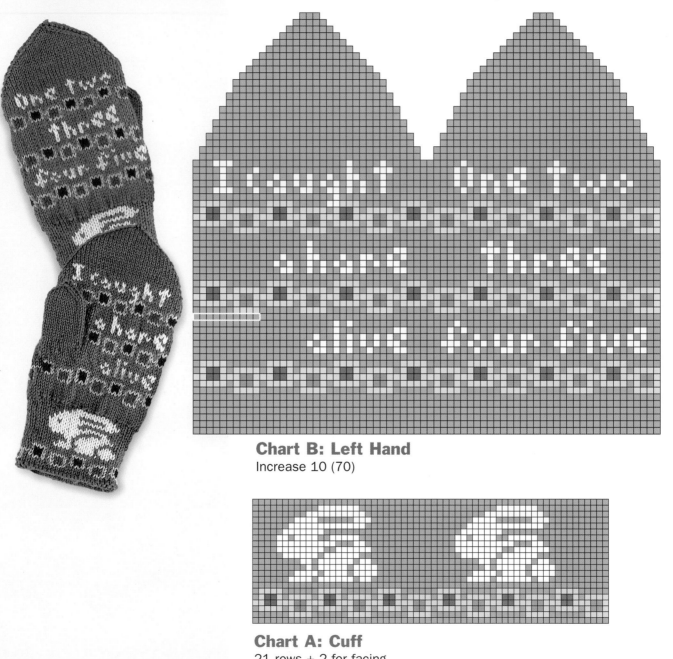

Chart B: Left Hand
Increase 10 (70)

Chart A: Cuff
21 rows + 2 for facing
Cast on 60

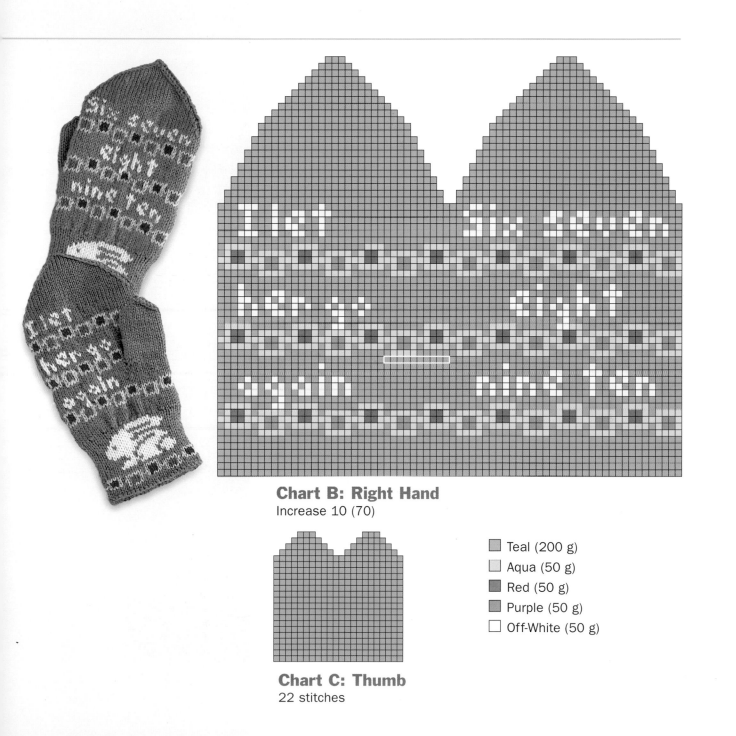

Chart B: Right Hand
Increase 10 (70)

Chart C: Thumb
22 stitches

■ Teal (200 g)
□ Aqua (50 g)
■ Red (50 g)
■ Purple (50 g)
□ Off-White (50 g)

Scarf

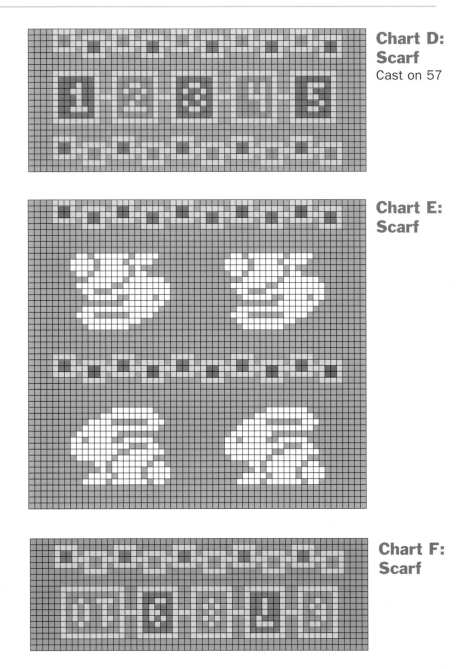

**Chart D:
Scarf**
Cast on 57

**Chart E:
Scarf**

**Chart F:
Scarf**

Design Tip

Here's another counting rhyme that you might want to try. Replace the rabbit icons with hens—see the hen icons in Hickety, Pickety on page 86.

*One, two, buckle my shoe
Three, four, knock at the door
Five, six, pick up sticks
Seven, eight, lay them straight
Nine, ten, a good fat hen*

Hat

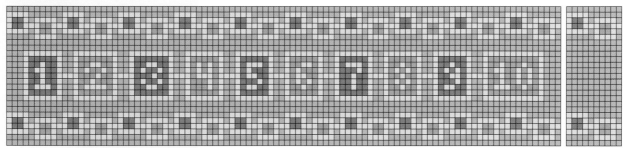

Chart G: Band

25 rows + 2 for facing
Cast on 180
(Note: Repeat the small section of the chart (above far right) 4 times before and after the longer section.)

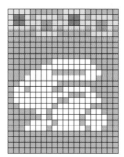

Chart H: Hat

No increase (180)

Design Tip

My first hat design was way too small. I was absolutely amazed at how large babies' heads are! To ensure a good fit, measure an existing hat that you know fits, and check your gauge by knitting a swatch of Chart G (the hat band). If your gauge isn't approximately 9 stitches to the inch (2.5 cm), adjust your needle size or modify the chart by increasing or decreasing the number of stitches. Pay attention to the number of repeats in the design. Counting Rhyme has a 10-stitch repeat, so add 10 stitches for every inch. Remember, the hat band will have a facing, making it double thick, so err on the side of too big versus too small.

Hickety, Pickety, My Black Hen

Hickety, pickety, my black hen
She lays eggs for gentlemen
Gentlemen come every day
To see what my black hen doth lay
Sometimes nine and sometimes ten
Hickety, pickety, my black hen

Hickety, Pickety, My Black Hen

This festive design—featuring hens and eggs amid banners of blue and green flags with yellow tips—is reminiscent of a county fair with all its old-fashioned charm. I started with a color scheme, then matched it with the verse. When I added black to the color scheme, because of the hens, it not only made a more congruent design, but offset the other colors dramatically.

Carmin Charen, age 5

Mittens

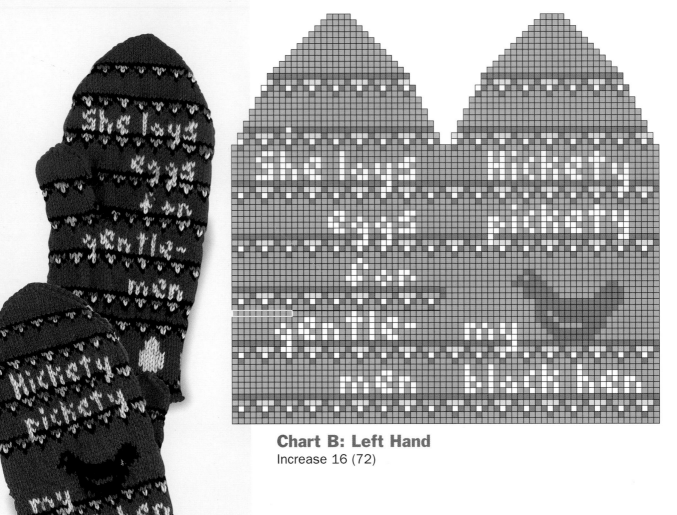

Chart B: Left Hand
Increase 16 (72)

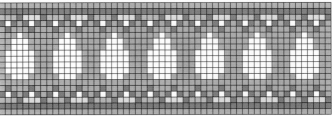

Chart A: Cuff
19 rows + 2 for facing
Cast on 56

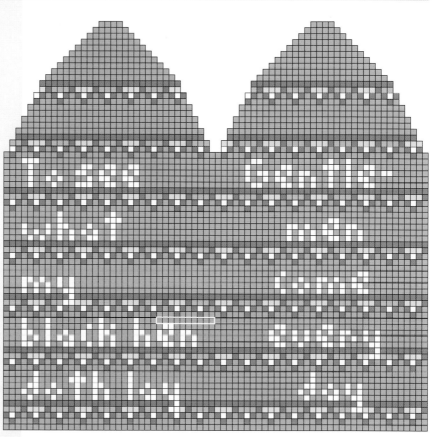

Chart B: Right Hand
Increase 16 (72)

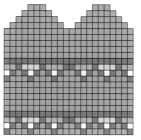

Chart C:
Left Thumb
22 stitches

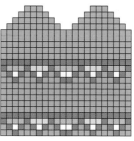

Chart C:
Right Thumb
22 stitches

■ Red (200 g)
■ Black (100 g)
■ Med. Blue (50 g)
□ Green (50 g)
□ Lt. Yellow (50 g)

Scarf

Chart D: Scarf
Cast on 57

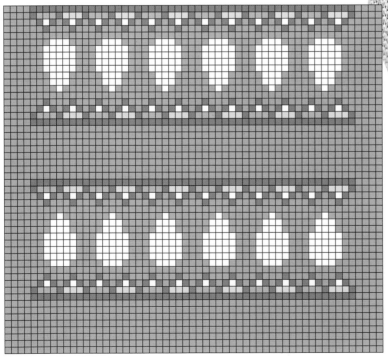

Chart E: Scarf

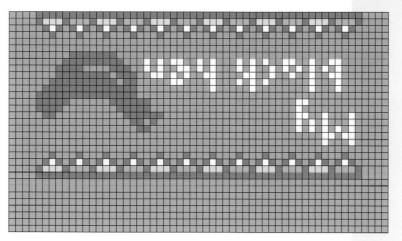

Chart F: Scarf

Hat

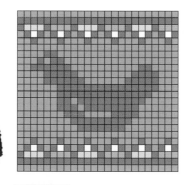

Chart G: Band
19 rows + 2 for facing
Cast on 168

Chart H: Hat
No increase (168)

Design Tip

To make a cord from which to attach a pompom or tassel from the top of a hat: Cut a piece of yarn approximately four times as long as you want the cord to be. Fold the yarn in half, looping the folded end around your index finger, and pinching the loose ends with the thumb and index finger of your other hand. Twist the looped end of the yarn until it is taut. Holding both ends securely, bring the two ends together, folding the cord in half. The tension will cause the yarn to twist into a cord. Sew a tassel or pompom to one end of the cord and sew the other end to the hat.

Wee Willie Winkie

Wee Willie Winkie
Runs through the town
Upstairs and downstairs
In his nightgown
Rapping at the window
Crying through the lock
Are the children in their beds?
For now it's eight o'clock

Wee Willie Winkie

Streetlights, stars, moons, and glowing houses warm this nightscape. I love the different perspectives—home, neighborhood, and world—united by the presence of light. The house border is no small feat! There are too many colors to carry across, so I cut 10-inch (25.5 cm) lengths of yarn for each house, allowing me to carry just the teal, black, and yellow. The border does take time and patience, but once you get past it, the solid blue stripes are a breeze.

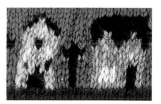

Jamonty Williams, age 10 months

Chart A: Main Blanket – Top
Cast on 186 stitches

■ Dk. Blue (100 g) ▨ Lavender (50 g)
▨ Teal (100 g) ▢ Aqua (50 g)
▢ Lt. Yellow (50 g) ▨ Black (50 g)
▢ Lt. Blue (50 g)

Design Tip
If you want to make the blanket longer, see the tip on page 47 for Sleep Baby Sleep.

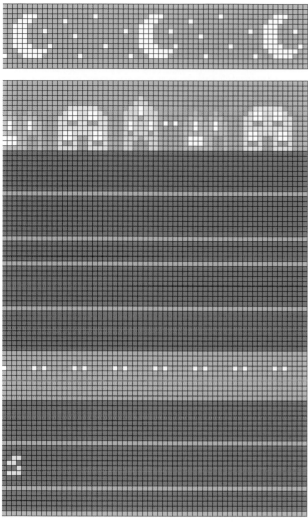

Design Tip

Reminder: Because there are so many lengths of yarn, you might want to cut 10-inch (25.5 cm) lengths of yarn for each house rather than carrying them across.

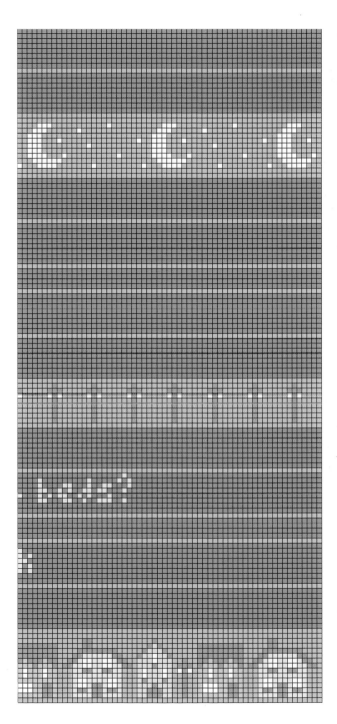

Chart A: Main Blanket – Bottom
Cast on 186

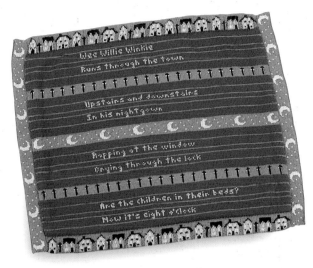

Favorite Night-Time Rhymes

I See the Moon
I see the moon
And the moon sees me
God bless the moon
And God bless me!

Star Light, Star Bright
Star light, star bright
First star I see tonight
I wish I may, I wish I might
Have the wish I wish tonight

Good Night, Sleep Tight
Good night, sleep tight
Wake up bright
In the morning light
To do what's right
With all your might

Three Little Kittens

Three little kittens
They lost their mittens
And they began to cry
Oh, mother, dear
We sadly fear
Our mittens we have lost!

What! Lost your mittens
You naughty kittens
Then you shall have no pie
Meow, meow
Then you shall have no pie

The three little kittens
They found their mittens
And they began to cry
Oh, mother, dear
See here, see here
Our mittens we have found!

What! Found your mittens
Then you're good kittens
And you shall have some pie
Purr-rr, purr-rr
Then you shall have some pie

Three Little Kittens

These mischievous kittens were designed in purple to contrast with the orange background. I used zigzag stripes to create a fun yet simple background, and

the clothesline border to add another dimension to the story. You might want to fasten these mittens onto a cord so that your "little kitten" won't lose them!

Evan Rhatigan, age 2½

Mittens

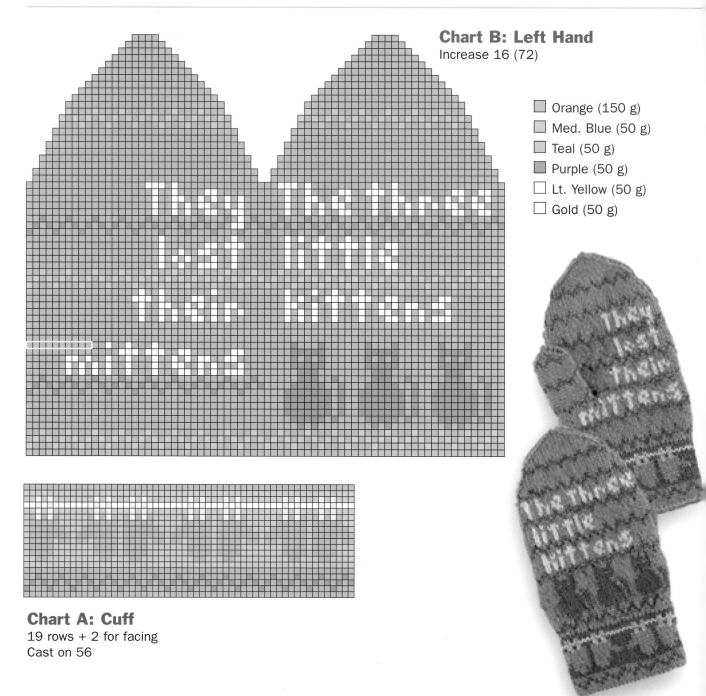

Chart B: Left Hand
Increase 16 (72)

- Orange (150 g)
- Med. Blue (50 g)
- Teal (50 g)
- Purple (50 g)
- Lt. Yellow (50 g)
- Gold (50 g)

Chart A: Cuff
19 rows + 2 for facing
Cast on 56

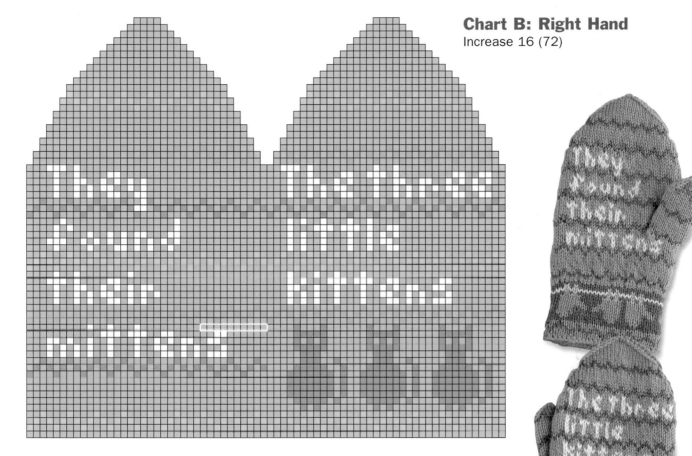

Chart B: Right Hand
Increase 16 (72)

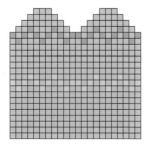

**Chart C:
Left Thumb**
22 stitches

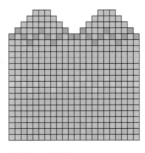

**Chart C:
Right Thumb**
22 stitches

Scarf

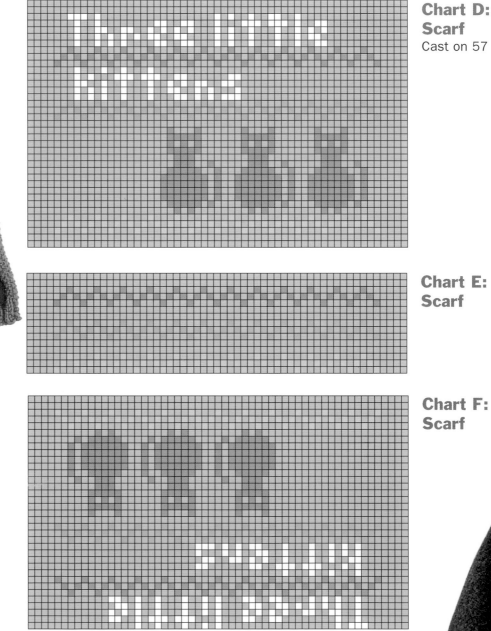

Chart D: Scarf
Cast on 57

Chart E: Scarf

Chart F: Scarf

Three Little Kittens
(continued)

*Three little kittens
Put on their mittens
And soon ate up the pie
Oh, mother, dear
We sadly fear
Our mittens we have
  soiled!*

*What! Soiled your mittens
You naughty kittens
And they began to sigh
Meow, meow
And they began to sigh*

Hat

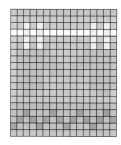

Chart G: Band
19 rows + 2 for facing
Cast on 176

Chart H: Hat
No increase (176)

Three Little Kittens (continued)

The three little kittens
They washed their mittens
And hung them out to dry
Oh, mother, dear
Do you not hear
Our mittens we have washed?

What! Washed your mittens
Then you're good kittens!
But I smell a rat close by
Meow, meow
We smell a rat close by

Lavender's Blue

Lavender's blue, dilly dilly
Lavender's green
When I am king, dilly dilly
You shall be queen

Call up your men, dilly dilly
Set them to work
Some to the plough, dilly dilly
Some to the cart

Some to make hay, dilly dilly
Some to thresh corn
While you and I, dilly dilly
Keep ourselves warm

Lavender's green, dilly dilly
Lavender's blue
If you love me, dilly dilly
I will love you!

Lavender's Blue

This sweet song with its promise of true love was the first song I learned to play on the piano. The blue-based colors are like a melody inspired by the words lavender, blue, and green. Thin vertical stripes bordering the crown motif peek between the heavier horizontal stripes, lending unity and playfulness. When I knitted the scarf, I carried the blue yarn across every row in order to keep the seed-stitch border all in blue; you could simplify it by having each border stitch match the color in its row.

Kayleigh Rhatigan, age 5

Mittens

■ Dk. Blue (150 g)
■ Purple (100 g)
■ Teal (50 g)
□ Lavender (50 g)

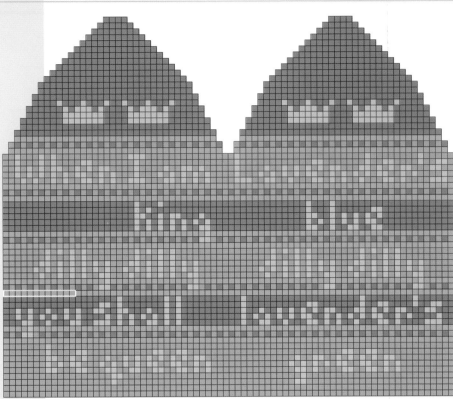

Chart B: Left Hand
Increase 20 (76)

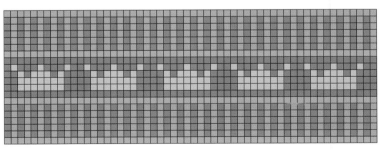

Chart A: Cuff
20 rows + 2 for facing
Cast on 56

Chart B: Right Hand
Increase 20 (76)

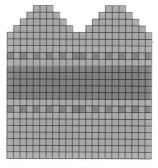

Chart C: Thumb
22 stitches

Lavender's Blue

Lavender's Blue is one of many popular folk songs for children. This one is based on a seventeenth-century ballad called "Diddle, Diddle," or "The Kind Country Lovers." The words "diddle, diddle" were later changed to "dilly dilly" as you see in the version I have selected.

Scarf

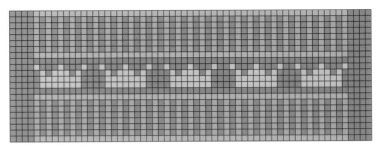

Chart D: Scarf
Cast on 61

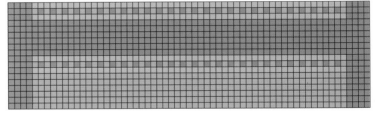

Chart E: Scarf

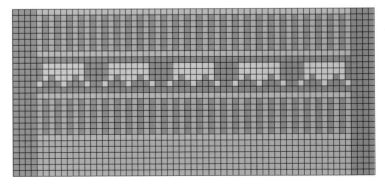

Chart F: Scarf

Design Tip

I love the pallet of blue-based colors in this design. If you prefer something livelier, make the crowns gold. If you like the colors, but are finding it too dark in general, use lighter hues, but make sure there is enough contrast between the two main colors and the one you will use for the words. For example, you could use lavender in place of purple and medium blue in place of dark blue; then use dark blue instead of lavender for the words.

Hat

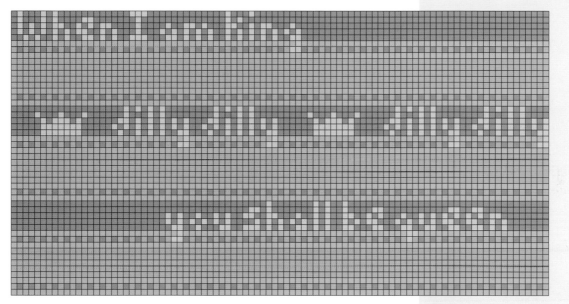

Chart G: Band
20 rows + 2 for facing
Cast on 176

Chart H: Hat
Increase 6 (182)

Itsy Bitsy Spider

The itsy bitsy spider
Went up the water spout
Down came the rain
And washed the spider out
Out came the sun
And dried up all the rain
And the itsy bitsy spider
Went up the spout again

Itsy Bitsy Spider

This dramatic design is a must for spider lovers or fans of the popular children's song. Patches of yellow and green act as spotlights, emphasizing black words and spiders on a red background. The mittens really tell the whole story: the spider climbing up the left hand, rain coming down the right. Be careful to twist your threads when transitioning between the yellow or green squares and the red background to prevent gaps from forming.

Alex Neel, age 2

Mittens

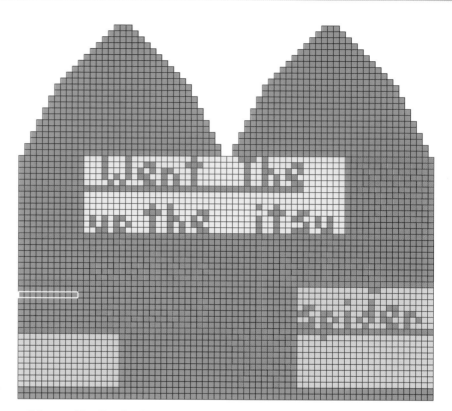

Chart B: Left Hand
Increase 22 (70)

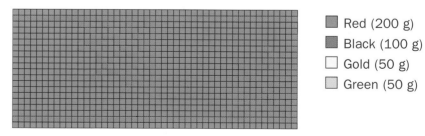

Chart A: Cuff
20 rows + 2 for facing
Cast on 48

■ Red (200 g)
■ Black (100 g)
□ Gold (50 g)
□ Green (50 g)

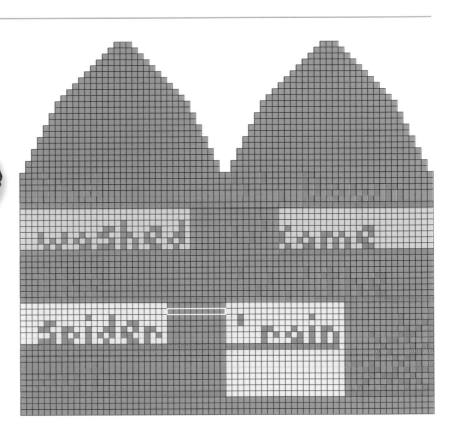

Chart B: Right Hand
Increase 22 (70)

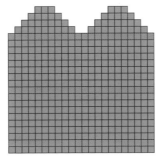

Chart C: Thumb
22 stitches

Design Tip

If you don't sew, a quick and simple
solution to mitten linings is to buy a
pair of those one-size-fits-all mittens
that stretch to fit (child-size, of course).
They're thin enough not to add bulk
and all you have to do is stitch them
into place. Be sure to read the
instructions for lining the mitten on
page 13; skip the first few steps and
go directly to the part about attaching
the lining.

Scarf

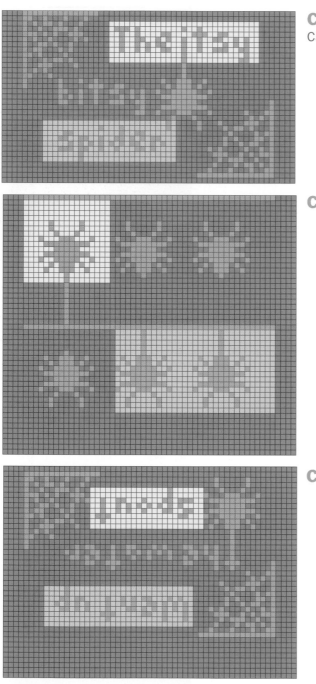

Chart D: Scarf
Cast on 57

Chart E: Scarf

Chart F: Scarf

Reading to Children

Nursery rhymes help build vocabulary and teach counting. They are fun to read out loud because they rhyme and have silly words like "itsy bitsy" and "hickety, pickety." It's natural to laugh and sing them, and of course children love to do that with you.

Hat

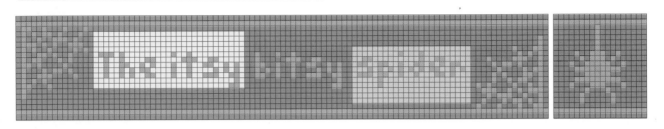

Chart G: Band

20 rows + 2 for facing
Cast on 175
(Note: Repeat the small section of the chart with the spider (above far right) 2 times before and after the longer section.)

Chart H: Hat

Increase 5 (180)

Reading to Children

To help reinforce learning, teachers use songs and finger plays (hand motions) with rhymes, especially those with up-and-down and "crawly" movements such as this one. The children's librarian at your local library can help you find books with such activities.

Queen of Hearts

The Queen of Hearts
She made some tarts
All on a summer's day

The Knave of Hearts
He stole the tarts
And took them clean away

The King of Hearts
Called for the tarts
And beat the knave full sore

The Knave of Hearts
Brought back the tarts
And vowed he'd steal no more

Queen of Hearts

I wanted to use purple as the base for a design, and a poem about royalty was a princess-perfect match. The rhyme inspired the crown-like four-pointed tassel hat in this and other designs, such as Lavender's Blue and Ring Around the Roses. The hat is easy to make, and the use of the Kitchener stitch gives a seamless appearance.

Emily White, age 4

Mittens

Purple (200 g)
Dk. Pink (200 g)
Med. Pink (50 g)
Off-White (50 g)

■ Purple (200 g)
■ Dk. Pink (200 g)
□ Med. Pink (50 g)
□ Off-White (50 g)

Chart B: Left Hand
Increase 20 (70)

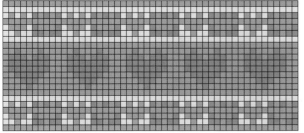

Chart A: Cuff
22 rows + 2 for facing
Cast on 50

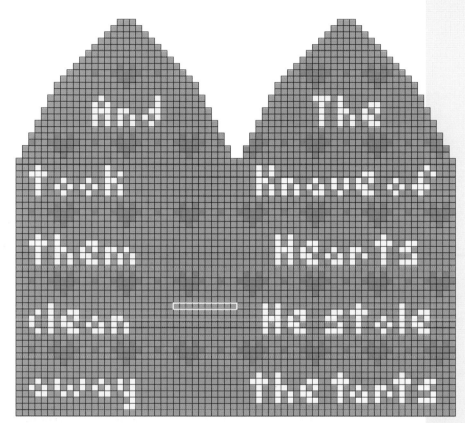

Chart B: Right Hand
Increase 20 (70)

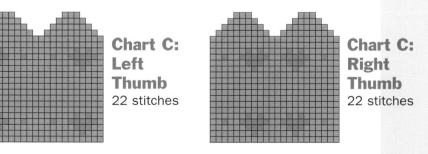

Chart C: Left Thumb
22 stitches

Chart C: Right Thumb
22 stitches

Scarf

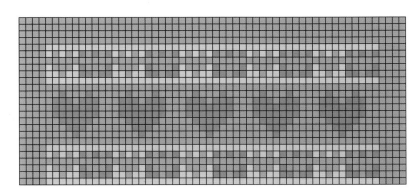

Chart D: Scarf
Cast on 58

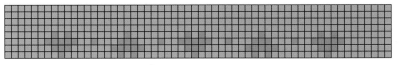

Chart E: Scarf

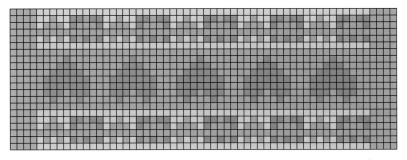

Chart F: Scarf

Queen of Hearts

Queen of Hearts was the name given to Elizabeth Stuart, Queen of Bohemia in the seventeenth century. Some say it was because of her beauty. Others say it was because of her resolute, charitable, and dignified manner. Elizabeth chose King Frederick of Winter as her husband and successor to the throne, but King Ferdinand, the "knave of hearts," stole the throne from Frederick, and Elizabeth and her family fled to Holland.

Hat

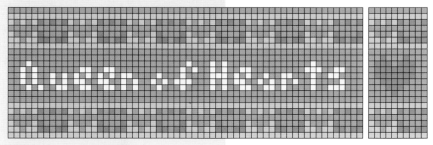

Chart G: Band

22 rows + 2 for facing
Cast on 180
(Note: Repeat the small section of the chart with the heart (above far right) 6 times before and after the longer section.)

Chart H: Hat

No increase (180)

Design Tip

Instead of purple and pink, consider making this project in pink and green (see Ring Around the Roses on page 34) or yellow and blue (see the Sleep Baby Sleep blanket on page 47).

Alphabet Song

A, B, C, D, E, F, G
H, I, J, K, L, M, N, O, P
Q, R, S, T, U, V
W, X, Y and Z
Now I know my ABCs
Next time won't you sing with me?

Alphabet Song

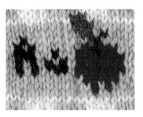

Who doesn't know the alphabet song? Some of us still sing it when filing! The design reminds me of the samplers young women used to make to exhibit their fine needlework skills. Because it features icons and motifs from designs throughout this book, the scarf is a bit of a sampler itself. This project is a good choice for the less experienced knitter. In fact, the scarf could be knit in just the background colors, and the pictures and letters added later using duplicate stitch.

Chavis Williams, age 5

Scarf

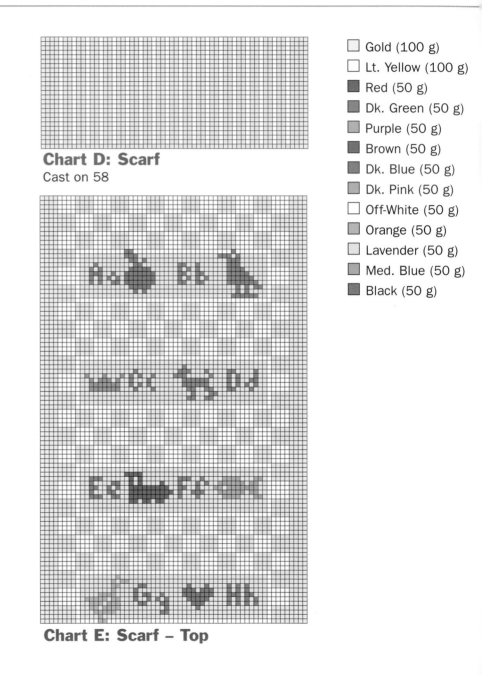

Chart D: Scarf
Cast on 58

Chart E: Scarf – Top

☐ Gold (100 g)
☐ Lt. Yellow (100 g)
■ Red (50 g)
■ Dk. Green (50 g)
■ Purple (50 g)
■ Brown (50 g)
■ Dk. Blue (50 g)
■ Dk. Pink (50 g)
☐ Off-White (50 g)
■ Orange (50 g)
☐ Lavender (50 g)
■ Med. Blue (50 g)
■ Black (50 g)

Design Tip

If you want to really try
your hand (and eye) at
design, try creating your
own baby blanket. Start
with a grid about 220
rows by 200 columns.
For a border, use a
simple checkerboard,
or letters of the alphabet,
or inscribe the first lines
of multiple nursery
rhymes. In the center
of the blanket, inscribe
your child's name and
date of birth.

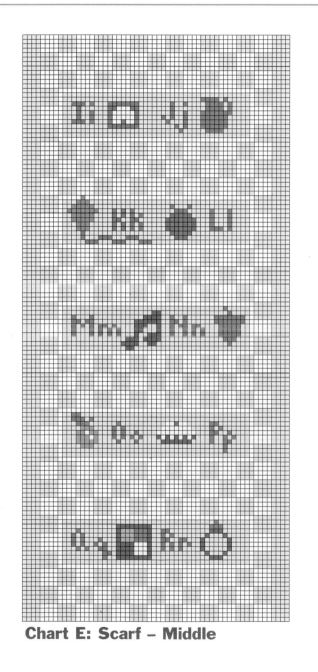

Chart E: Scarf – Middle

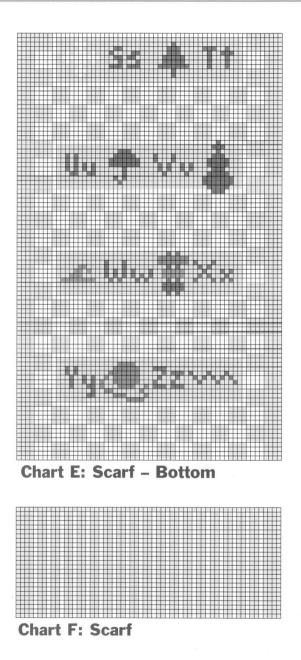

Chart E: Scarf – Bottom

Chart F: Scarf

Hat

Chart G: Band
20 rows + 2 for facing
Cast on 180

Chart H: Hat
Increase 4 (184)

Design Tip

I chose two shades of yellow for the checkered background of this design, but you could easily substitute your child's favorite color. If you decide to use two different colors, try complementary colors in tones that offer a subtle contrast. Here are some suggestions:

- ☐ Lt. Green and ☐ Lt. Blue
- ☐ Lt. Yellow and ☐ Green
- ☐ Pink and ☐ Lavender
- ☐ Lt. Peach and ☐ Lt. Green

Keep in mind you may need to substitute other colors for the pictures on the scarf if they don't stand out against your new background.

Alphabet Chart

Acknowledgments

I wish to thank the following people for lending their careful attention to the design, quality, and accuracy of the patterns in this book, and for their generous donation of time and needlework skills: Shelly Britton, Tina Cronin, Tammy Hagan, Amy Jabas, Suzanne Merideth, Carol Michaels, and Melissa Suek.

Thanks to the finishing crew: Shelly Britton, Jill Claggett, Andy Clark, Beth Clark, Linda Ehli, Marcia Engeltjes, Tammy Hagan, Sara Kloepper, Suzanne Merideth, Sheryl Schwen, Joanne Pfau, Michelle Teske, and Brenda VanDyke.

Special thanks to my head and hand models: Maddie Bernard, Lexi Cronin, Taylor Cronin, and Hanna Hagan. And to the children who appear in the photographs: Jaxon Banks, Carmin Charen, Margaret Rose Murphy, Alex Neel, Evan Neel, Evan Rhatigan, Kayleigh Rhatigan, Maggie Rhatigan, Emily White, Chavis Williams, and Jamonty Williams.

Finally, thanks to my editor, Marcianne Miller; art director, Stacey Budge; photographer, Sandra Stambaugh; illustrator, Dana Irwin; and all the folks at Lark Books whose diligent work and artistry produced the most beautiful book I could have wished for.

A Note About Suppliers

Usually, the supplies you need for knitting the projects in Lark books can be found at your local yarn shop or craft supply store. Occasionally, however, you may need to buy materials or tools from specialty suppliers. In order to provide you with the most up-to-date information, we have created a listing of suppliers on our web site, which we update on a regular basis. Visit us at www.larkbooks.com, click on "Craft Supply Sources," and then click on the relevant topic. You will find numerous companies listed with their web address and/or mailing address and phone number.

Index